inside

ABOUT ME

Start off by focusing on who you are, what your personality is like and what is important to you.

Getting started
Getting the picture
Getting it down
Getting some answers
Getting to know me
Getting heard
Getting down to it

HOBBIES AND INTERESTS

Discover activities that you might enjoy and think about how to develop your talents and skills.

Getting interested
Getting involved
Getting out

FAMILY AND HOME

Think about the people you live with, the responsibilities in your house and the space you call home.

Getting together
Getting noticed
Getting the picture
Getting inside
Getting along
Getting responsible
Getting all you need
Getting it
Jo & Joey

FRIENDS

Have a look at friendships and think about how to make them even better.

Getting to know you
Getting on
Getting acquainted
Getting along
Getting it right
Getting tough
Getting it out
Getting the message
Getting over it
Getting it across
Jo & Joey

SCHOOL

Work out why school is important and how to make the most of your education.

Getting it straight
Getting wise
Getting to grips
Getting the idea
Getting clued up
Getting in line
Getting done
Getting organised
Getting ready
Getting it all in
Getting it under control
Getting worked up
Jo & Joey

S

Sense your mood and decide how to work with your emotions.

Getting in the mood
Getting dizzy
Getting happy
Getting a smile
Getting down
Getting upset
Getting scared
Getting goosebumps
Getting mad
Getting on with it
Getting hot
Getting cool
Getting that feeling
Getting it fixed
Getting it sorted
Getting help

THE FUTURE

Decide how the future might be for you.

Getting ahead
Getting a helping hand
Getting the picture

RECORD

Keep a record of your achievements.

Getting real
Getting better
Hurrah

ABOUT ME

my best...

Food:

Book:

Friend:

Music:

Hobby:

Subject:

Other things I like:

note — Have a go at filling in the boxes to record all about you!

my worst...

Nightmare:

Memory:

Phobia:

Subject:

Food:

Habit:

Other things I dislike:

stuff

ABOUT ME

getting the picture

Draw a picture of yourself!

In this picture, I am...

ABOUT ME

getting it down

Dear Me,

Tell yourself what it is like to be you or write about a typical day in your life!

From Me

getting some answers

How do you think?
Write your responses!

If I were an animal, I'd be a

> If I was a superhero, my special power would be

If I could change one thing about me, it would be

> If I could be someone else for one day, I would be

If I was granted a wish, it would be

> I find it difficult to

It upsets me when

> I wish I was allowed to

Something you might not know about me is

> The thing I treasure most is

If I had a million pounds, I would

My favourite teacher is

My best piece of advice is

I'm scared of

My most embarrassing moment was

If I could make a 30-second call to anyone, it would be

I couldn't live without

If I ruled the world, I would

I get mad when

My earliest memory is

A person I admire is

It makes me happy when

getting to know me

ABOUT ME

If you were a recipe, what ingredients would you contain?

friendliness

getting heard

ABOUT ME

Draw or write about the most important things in the world to you!

getting down to it

ABOUT ME

Discuss your responses with a friend or adult.

	yep	sort of	nope

myself

- Can you give three reasons why it's good to be you?
- Can you say something that you are good at and explain why?
- Can you say something that you are not so good at and explain why?

classroom

- Can you describe (or show) how you'd let your teacher know you are listening?
- Can you think of three school rules and say why each one is important?
- Can you talk about something you have learnt this week?

friends

- Can you give two reasons why you are a good friend and one thing that would make you an even better friend?
- Can you describe what you would do if your friend was crying and explain why?
- Can you suggest two things that you could do if you were being teased?

	yep	sort of	nope
feelings			
Can you name three different feelings and discuss when you have felt them?			
Can you explain how you could tell that someone else was feeling sad?			
Can you give two ways that might help calm you down if you were feeling angry?			
solving			
Can you explain what you could do if you got stuck on your homework?			
Can you suggest two things you might do if you and a friend couldn't agree which game to play?			
Can you explain what you would do if you couldn't find your P.E. kit?			
attitude			
Can you think of three reasons why you should come to school?			
Can you explain what you would do if you thought your partner was wrong?			
Can you say one school rule you agree with and why and one you would change and why?			

HOBBIES & INTERESTS

getting interested

What do you like to do in your spare time?
Need some ideas? Try thinking of an activity that's...

creative

physical

on your own

in a team

using a talent

relaxing

adventurous

learning new skills

I've decided to try out...

getting involved

HOBBIES & INTERESTS

Find out what clubs and teams your school has!

Write down the name of a friend who is a member of each club!

Monday	
	Why do they go to this club?
Tuesday	
	What is it like at this club?
Wednesday	
	What will they be doing at the club this week?
Thursday	
	What's the best thing about this club?
Friday	
	What do they do at this club?

The club I'd like to try out is...

getting out

HOBBIES & INTERESTS

Design a poster to advertise your club or hobby!

Remember!
What is the club/team/hobby?
What's so great about it?
Who can join in?
Where and when are the meetings held?
What do you need to bring along?
Does it cost anything to have a go?

getting together

FAMILY & HOME

How many different roles do you play in your life?

Are you a sister or brother, a friend or helper, a son or daughter?

I'm a... Pupil

Helper

Friend

Brother

Neighbour

Carer

Your favourite role and why?

Your least favourite role and why?

getting noticed

FAMILY & HOME

What would these people say is your best quality?

What would these people say they like least about you?

thumbs up

Family Member

thumbs down

Why might this person think this?

thumbs up

Friend

thumbs down

Why might this person think this?

thumbs up

Teacher

thumbs down

Why might this person think this?

getting the picture

FAMILY & HOME

Draw a picture of your family!

What things do you do together as a family?

getting inside

FAMILY & HOME

What's it like where you live?

My home is a

I have lived here for

I live there with

My room is

From my window, I can see

At home I can

At home I can't

The room I do my homework in is

What I like about my home is

What I don't like about my home is

Home is

getting along

FAMILY & HOME

What's it like living with you? Tick the boxes that sound like you!

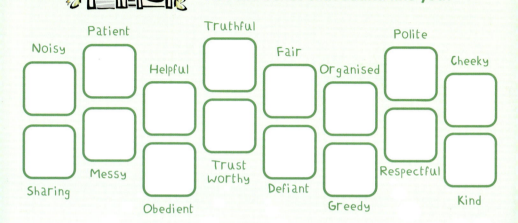

- Noisy
- Patient
- Helpful
- Truthful
- Fair
- Organised
- Polite
- Cheeky
- Sharing
- Messy
- Obedient
- Trustworthy
- Defiant
- Greedy
- Respectful
- Kind

Do you usually do what you are told?

Can people rely on you?

Would you still do something even if you were told not to?

Do you care about other people's feelings and their belongings?

What's the best thing for others about living with you?

What's the worst thing for others about living with you?

What will you do to make it easier for those you live with?

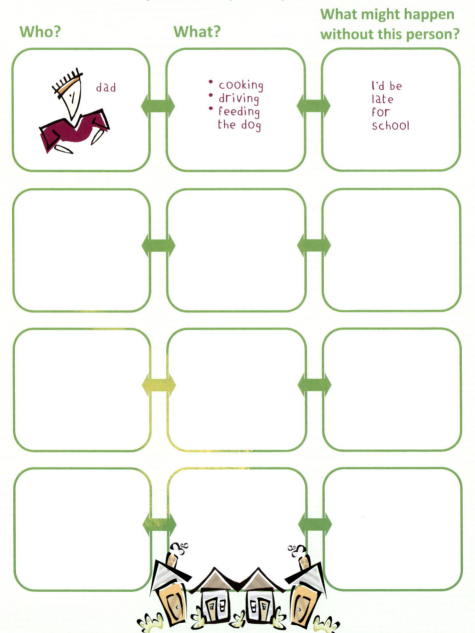

What do you do?

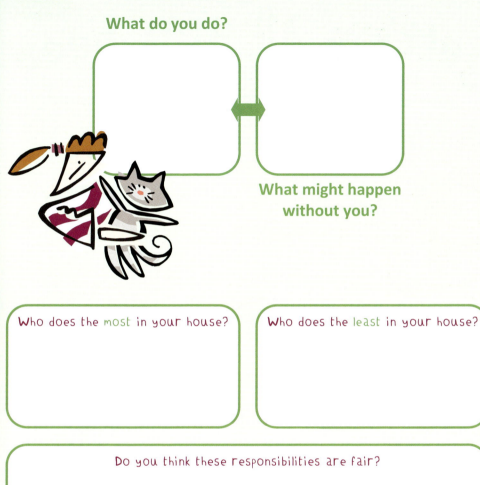

What might happen without you?

Who does the most in your house?

Who does the least in your house?

Do you think these responsibilities are fair?

What would make things fairer?

getting all you need

FAMILY & HOME

What do these animals, plants and humans need to live?

A dog needs:

A plant needs:

My mum/dad/carer needs:

My teacher needs:

A friend who is upset needs:

I need:

FAMILY & HOME

getting it

What happens in your house?

The rules in our home are:

Try creating some rules for your bedroom but remember, if you share a room, you may have to negotiate!

Turn your rules into a poster for your bedroom door!

Jo & Joey

FAMILY & HOME

Here's a common situation...

Jo: Hey Joey! What's up?

Joey: Sob! Sniff! I can't do my homework!

Jo: Huh? Why not?

Joey: Because my little sister is being annoying! She's always in my room!

Jo: She just likes hanging out with you, Joey!

Joey: I know but she also wants to play on the computer! I need it for the homework!

Jo: So you don't want to upset your sister or our teacher!

Joey: Exactly! What should I do?

getting to know you

FRIENDS

What ingredients would you put into a recipe for friendship?

good listener

getting on

FRIENDS

What kind of friend are you?
Try this quiz for fun to find out!

Which one of these words best describes you?

Outgoing   **Reliable**   **Independent**

- Do you have a big group of friends?
- Do you have one or two close friends?
- Do you prefer your own company?

- Do your friends have similar hobbies & interests?
- Do you often try to make people laugh?
- Do your friends often hang around with others?
- Do your friends share their secrets with you?

- Do you usually stick with same group?
- Do you enjoy working in a team?
- Can you easily start a conversation with someone?
- Is it important to you to have friends?
- Do you prefer doing things on your own?

Busy Bee
You probably have a big crowd of friends who you tend to stick with. You're a real team player and are great at sharing and joining in.

For making a best friend, try finding out who is the most similar to you.

Social Butterfly
You have lots of friends but float around, choosing different friends each day. You are sociable and try hard to please others but are not sure who to trust.

For friends who are always there, try joining a team at your school.

Faithful Hound
You are likely to have a few carefully selected close friends. You're reliable and trustworthy but perhaps can be shy around new people.

To feel confident around new people, try inviting just one new person to join in a game with your friends.

Solitary Sole
You are independent and enjoy your own company. You probably don't like team games and can be nervous around other people.

To meet new friends with similar interests, try joining a school club or team!

getting acquainted

FRIENDS

See what you can find out about your classmates!

Write down the name of someone who...

...travels to school in the same way as you:

...shares the same favourite subject as you:

...plays a musical instrument:

...speaks another language:

...has a different hobby to you:

What would life be like if everyone was exactly the same?

FRIENDS

getting along

What would you do in these friendship dilemmas?

You've lost something you borrowed from your friend.

You and your best friend both entered a competition and she won.

Your teacher asks you about a fight that happened at lunchtime, outside in the playground. You know who started it but he's your best friend and you are worried about telling on him and getting him into trouble.

You overhear someone being nasty about your friend.

You see your friend going through a bag in the cloakroom which doesn't belong to him.

You haven't received an invitation to a friend's party.

You read your friend's secret diary and it says something mean about you.

You suspect that your friend has told other people your secret.

getting it right

What might these friends be saying?

getting tough

FRIENDS

...and what might these **bullies** be saying?

getting it out

FRIENDS

What could you say to join in the conversation?

"That film was rubbish!"

"Yeah, shame about the rest of it!"

"I really liked the very end bit though!"

"Hope the neighbours don't complain about the loud music!"

"It's a great disco though! Look, I bought this new T-shirt to wear!"

Top Tips!

Make eye contact!

Listen!

Ask a question!

Say something nice!

Smile!

FRIENDS

getting the message

How well do you listen?

Listening is one of the most important skills in any friendship.

Write down two ways you can tell that someone isn't listening.

Make a note of two conversations. Tick the boxes to see how well you both listened.

Friend A	You	Friend B	You	
☐	☐	☐	☐	Gave full attention
☐	☐	☐	☐	Made eye contact
☐	☐	☐	☐	Nodded occasionally/said "Uh-huh" or "Yeah"
☐	☐	☐	☐	Didn't interrupt
☐	☐	☐	☐	Respected each other's opinion
☐	☐	☐	☐	Asked relevant questions
☐	☐	☐	☐	Reflected back in own words

How will you improve your listening skills next time?

FRIENDS

getting over it

Sometimes we have arguments with our friends. Try to work through the situation using these suggestions.

Solving a dispute

Decide on a safe and sensible time and place to discuss things.

Stay calm and don't get aggressive as the other person will not want to listen to you.

Make sure that everyone has a turn to speak and is listened to.

Apologise for your part in the conflict. This might also encourage others to apologise too.

Make positive suggestions about how to improve the situation and listen to others' suggestions too.

Ask someone neutral to be there to mediate if you think it might help.

Make a joint agreement about what should happen next and make sure you stick to it.

Good Luck!

1. What is happening or has happened?
2. How does it make me feel and why?
3. Why might this be happening?
4. How have I hindered this situation?
5. How have I already tried to solve this problem?
6. Why do I want things to change?
7. What could I/we try next?
8. How could we avoid this in the future?
9. What will I do next to help solve this dispute?
10. Who can I ask for help?

FRIENDS

getting it across

Things aren't always as straight forward as they first seem.
What do you think about these scenarios?

Jordan

overhears a gang saying something nasty about his best mate. He tells his best mate what the boys were saying about him because he thinks he should know.

Jordan should tell his best mate what was said.

Strongly Agree | Agree | Not Sure | Disagree | Strongly Disagree

Why?

Becky

buys a magazine at the shop and pays at the counter. The shop assistant gives her too much change. She decides not to tell him and keep the extra money.

Becky shouldn't admit to the extra change.

Strongly Agree | Agree | Not Sure | Disagree | Strongly Disagree

Why?

Joshua

is being forced by some older kids to do something he doesn't want to do. He decides to do it because he doesn't want to get beaten up.

Joshua should do as the older kids tell him.

Strongly Agree | Agree | Not Sure | Disagree | Strongly Disagree

Why?

Sandeep really wants to buy a birthday present for her mum as a special surprise. She lies about where she is going so that she can keep it a secret.

Sandeep should lie.

Strongly Agree | Agree | Not Sure | Disagree | **Strongly Disagree**

Why?

Chelsea thinks her best friend's new hair cut is unflattering and untrendy. She doesn't want to tell a lie so she tells her best friend what she truly thinks.

Chelsea should tell her friend the truth.

Strongly Agree | Agree | Not Sure | Disagree | Strongly Disagree

Why?

Lee is worried about a friend who told him a secret and begged him not to tell. Lee thinks his friend may be in danger but he doesn't tell a soul.

Lee should keep quiet.

Strongly Agree | Agree | **Not Sure** | Disagree | Strongly Disagree

Why?

Write about a time when you had to make a hard decision...

FRIENDS

Jo & Joey

Here's a common situation...

Hey Jo! What's up?

My mum says I can't come to the fun fair with you guys on Saturday!

Oh no! That's disappointing! Why not?

Because it's my sister's birthday!

Well, birthdays are special and your sister will be upset if you're not there!

Yeah, I know. I wish there was a way I could be in both places at once!

Hmm... I know what you mean. We'll think of something!

Look at the poster! I don't want to miss out on all the fun!

What could Joey suggest to Jo?

Fun Fair!

All Weekend:
Saturday & Sunday

At:
Green Park

*Only £4.00

Poor Jo! What can I suggest?

Why do you think this?

getting it straight

SCHOOL

What do you think about school?

Things I am good at:

Things I'd like to improve at:

What I like best about school:

What I like least about school:

I learn best when:

I'm bored when:

I come to school for:

School would be better if:

As Head Teacher, I would:

getting wise

SCHOOL

Try this quiz to discover your preferred learning style!

1. In a lesson, I prefer the teacher to:

 Do a demonstration

 Write or draw on the board

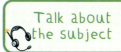 Talk about the subject

2. I follow instructions best when:

 Someone tells me

 Someone shows me

 They are written

3. In my spare time, I enjoy:

 Watching TV

 Listening to music

 Playing a game

4. After meeting someone for the first time, I am most likely to:

 What they were doing

 What they looked like

What they were saying

5. If I could choose, I'd rather take part in:

 A Music lesson

 An Art lesson

 A P.E. lesson

6. I enjoy stories best when:

 I act it out

 Someone reads it aloud

 I read it myself

---

Mostly
SEE You learn best by *watching*. Make sure you can see the board.

Mostly
HEAR You learn best by *listening*. Be sure to ask questions if you need to.

Mostly
DO You learn best by *trying things out*. Make use of any equipment.

getting to grips

SCHOOL

Think of some of the adults and pupils at school.
What jobs do they do?

Midday supervisor
• Organising lunchtime
• Helping in the playground

What about you?

What are your responsibilities at school?

getting the idea

SCHOOL

How would you deal with these distractions?

Your neighbours want you to come out to play but you've got homework to do!

A boy behind you in class keeps kicking you whilst you are working!

You are in assembly and your friend wants to tell you about her holiday!

You had a bad night's sleep and are worrying about what's going on at home.

What's your biggest distraction?

How do you deal with this?

getting clued up

SCHOOL

Ever wondered why you have to come to school and learn?

Let's think about some different jobs that people do...	Which subjects might they need to know about to do their job well?	What might happen if this person doesn't pay attention in their lessons?
 Teacher		
 Vet	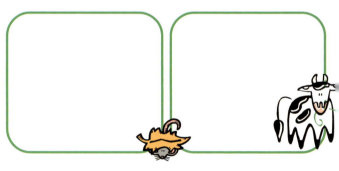	
 Footballer	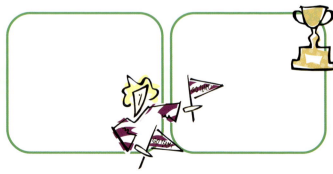	

getting in line

SCHOOL

Pretend that you are the new Head Teacher and imagine that you are changing the rules in your school!

Which rules do you agree with?

Rule:

Why?

Rule:

Why?

Rule:

Why?

Which rules do you disagree with?

Rule:

Why?

Rule:

Why?

Which rules would you add?

Rule:

Why?

Rule:

Why?

getting done

SCHOOL

If you broke these rules, what consequences would you face at your school?

Being late:

Bullying in the playground:

Talking when you shouldn't be:

Not using the lollipop person to cross the road:

Do you think these punishments are fair?

Chewing gum in class:

Not doing or not handing in your homework:

Copying someone else's work:

Not playing by the rules in a game:

Stealing:

Why do you think we need rules and punishments?

SCHOOL

getting organised

How organised are you?

In the morning before school, do you wake up to:

- ★ the sound of your alarm clock which you set the night before
- ★ the sound of your family getting up - it's usually about the right time
- ★ your mum yelling at you to get up or else you'll be late again

Your first lesson of the day is P.E. You:

- ★ get changed quickly and start warming up
- ★ change into your stinky kit which hasn't been washed for a while
- ★ have to sit and watch because you forgot your kit

You are a member of a lunchtime club. You:

- ★ check your watch and turn up five minutes early
- ★ wait for a dinner lady to remind you and turn up just in time
- ★ were too busy with your mates, you missed the club altogether

You have some homework to complete. You:

- ★ write it in your homework diary, do it and hand it in on time
- ★ write it on scrap paper, do it, then hand it in a day late
- ★ forget to write it down, forget to do it, forget to hand it in

You've been invited to a party. You:

- ★ turn up on time together with a present and card
- ★ call your friend to check where it is because you lost the invitation
- ★ forget

★ **Mostly Green**
Super organised!
You're usually on time
and in the right place!
Well done!

★ **Mostly Orange**
Need to improve!
Write a 'To Do' list then
decide which jobs are most
important and do them first!

★ **Mostly Purple**
Disorganised!
Use a diary and a watch!
Tidy up your desk/room/bag so
you know where things are!

SCHOOL

getting ready

Ready to test your memory?

The aim of this game is to see how many items you can remember without looking!

Give yourself one minute to memorise the items!

Tip:
Try picturing each object with a person you know!
(Granny scared of the mouse...)

Tip:
Try creating a silly story linking all the items in some way!
(Michael the mouse lived in a shell...)

Tip:
Try putting a tune, rhythm or even just funny sounds to each item!
(Snip! Scissors!)

Now you can use these tips to remember other things too such as friends' birthdays, spellings, or items on a shopping list!

getting it all in

SCHOOL

Be prepared to get organised!
What might these people need to pack in their bags?

Preston's Bag
School day trip to the seaside

Preston might need:

Jo's Bag
Shopping in town with her sister

Jo might need:

Sean's Bag
His dad's house overnight

Sean might need:

How can you tell that someone is organised?

getting it under control

SCHOOL

Write down which subjects you have on each day!

Write down what you will need on each day!

Monday

Tuesday

Wednesday

Thursday

Friday

Use this chart as a reminder when packing your bag (the night before)!

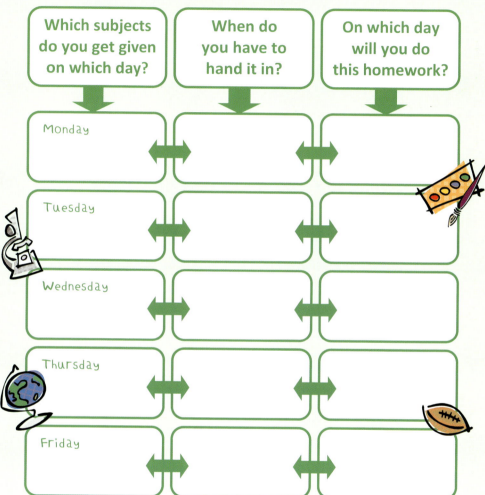

SCHOOL

Jo & Joey

Here's a common situation...

Hey Joey! What's up?

Sob! Sniff! I can't tell you, Jo!

Huh? Why not?

That gang from the year above said they'd beat me up if I did!

That sounds awful! You can tell *me*, can't you?

Well, if I tell you, will you promise not to tell anyone else?

I'll try... but you're in danger, Joey!

What?! You must be terrified!

They stole my lunch money and called me names! Sob! They said they're going to get me tonight!

What could Jo suggest to Joey?

Why do you think this?

getting in the mood

FEELINGS

How are you feeling right now? Why?
What do you think these people are feeling?

Pick a feeling and talk about when you've felt that way.

getting dizzy

FEELINGS

**How many different feelings can you think of?
Get your friends to help you!**

On your marks! Get set! Go!

Hint!
There may be more than one word for the same/similar feeling!

Grand total

Tick all the feelings you have felt!

getting happy

FEELINGS

What does happiness feel like?

Draw what happens to your body when you feel happy!

Sometimes, happiness is made up of other feelings.

What do you think these other feelings might be?

getting a smile

FEELINGS

Record your happy thoughts!

A person that makes me feel happy:

A place that makes me feel happy:

A memory that makes me feel happy:

A time of year that makes me feel happy:

A song that makes me feel happy:

An object that makes me feel happy:

Something I like doing that makes me feel happy:

The thing that makes me happiest of all:

The thing that might make me even happier:

getting down

FEELINGS

What does sadness feel like?

Draw what happens to your body when you feel sad!

Sometimes, sadness is made up of other feelings.

What do you think these other feelings might be?

getting upset

FEELINGS

What makes you feel sad?

sad

sadder

saddest

What helps you feel better when you feel sad?

events
memories
situations
people
stories
places

getting scared

FEELINGS

What does fear feel like?

Draw what happens to your body when you feel scared!

Sometimes, fear is made up of other feelings.

What do you think these other feelings might be?

getting goosebumps

FEELINGS

Try drawing some of the things that you are afraid of!

Now try drawing yourself overcoming one of your fears!

FEELINGS

getting on with it

How do you deal with anger?

Strategies

Talk to a friend
Swear
Fight
Take deep breaths
Be alone
Ignore it
Say how you feel
Gang up
Plan revenge
Apologise
Insult
Run away
Walk away
Shout
Turn it into a joke
Stay calm
Talk to an adult
Be neutral
Write it down
Stay away from school
Do something relaxing
Listen
Count to ten

Cross the strategies for dealing with anger that are likely to make you feel **more** angry.

Any others?

Tick the strategies for dealing with anger that are likely to make you feel **less** angry.

Any others?

Always think: Will this make me more angry or less angry?

getting hot

FEELINGS

What makes you feel angry?

> Absolutely fuming!!!!

> Very angry!!!

> Quite annoyed!!

> A bit grumpy!
>
> **Start here...**

What makes you lose it. lose it. lose it?!

getting cool

FEELINGS

What things can you do to help you calm down?

Cooling down!

Start here...

Quite chilly!!

Getting cold!!!

Freezing!!!!

What makes you calm, calmer, calmest?

getting that feeling

Over a day or a even a week, record your feelings and draw a face to match. What made you feel this way?

Feeling

Feeling

Feeling

Feeling

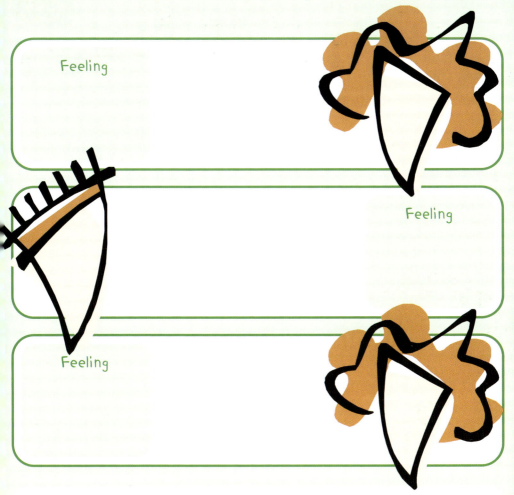

Feeling

Feeling

Feeling

Which feeling did you like most and why?

Which feeling did you like least and why?

FEELINGS

getting it fixed

What advice would you give the people below?

I'm worried about what my mum will say when she finds out I was fighting in the playground and had to stay in at lunchtime for detention.

I'm worried about a girl in my class. She always steals my packed lunch because she doesn't have one of her own.

Whose advice do you trust?

getting it sorted

FEELINGS

Got a problem? No problem! Write it down and then list three different possible solutions and what you think might happen on each route...

So, what's up?

1

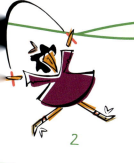

2

3

getting help

FEELINGS

Who can help you with what?
Link each problem with the person or people who could help.

Teacher

Parents/Carers

School Nurse

Feeling sick	Feeling left out	Teasing
Forgotten lunch	Playground fight	Homework
Finding £20	Feeling scared	Family row

Friend

Learning Mentor

Brother/Sister

Who else could you ask for help if you needed it?

getting ahead

FUTURE

How do you imagine your future?

I would like...

To be

To have

To find out

To learn

To see

To know

To remember

getting a helping hand

FUTURE

Write down five things that you will need to do so that you can achieve your dreams...

Action Point 1:

Action Point 2:

Action Point 3:

Action Point 4:

Action Point 5:

Your future is in your hands!

getting the picture

FUTURE

Draw a picture to show how you see yourself in the future!

In this picture, I am...

RECORD

getting real

Record your achievements here!

Remind yourself of your achievements whenever you feel 'down in the dumps'!

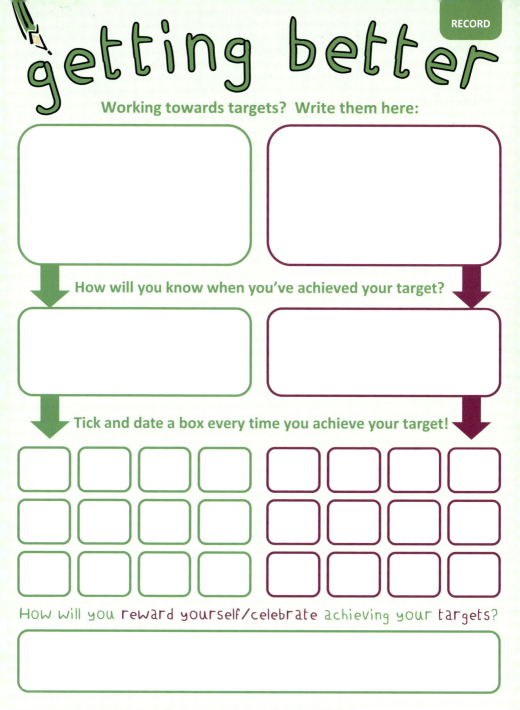

hurrah

You've completed 'Feeling Fabulous'!

What have you learnt about yourself?

What have you learnt about others?

What advice would you give others like you?

What positive change will you start making to your life today?

How would you describe the 'new' you?